fast thinking: work overload

PEARSON EDUCATION LIMITED
Head Office:
Edinburgh Gate
Harlow CM20 2JE
Tel: +44 (0)1279 623623
Fax: +44 (0)1279 431059

London Office:
128 Long Acre
London WC2E 9AN
Tel: +44 (0)20 7447 2000
Fax: +44 (0)20 7240 5771
Website: www.business-minds.com

First published in Great Britain in 2001

ISBN 0 273 65315 6

British Library Cataloguing in Publication Data
A CIP catalogue record for this book can be obtained from the British Library

10 9 8 7 6 5 4 3 2 1

Typeset by Pantek Arts Ltd, Maidstone, Kent.
Printed and bound in Great Britain by Ashford Colour Press, Hampshire

The Publishers' policy is to use paper manufactured from sustainable forests.

fast thinking: work overload

- create more time
- tackle the backlog
- clear your desk

by Ros Jay

contents

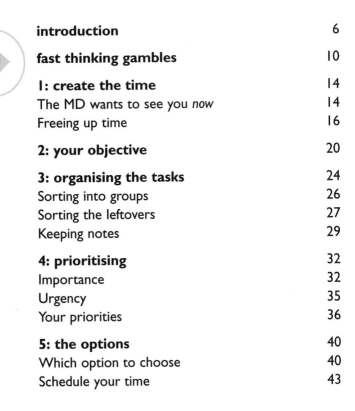

introduction

Your in-tray is the height of a small tower block, you can't find your phone under the pile of to-do lists and post-it notes, your boss wants to see you in five minutes, you're due at a vital meeting in a quarter of an hour, and reception has just called to tell you there is a visitor to see you now.

Familiar? If you are one of the millions of people for whom work is always so frantic that there's no time to catch up with yourself, this is the book for you. There's plenty of advice around (much of it plain unrealistic) on how to make sure you never build up a backlog, but it's too late for all that. You've got the backlog *now*, and the only question you need answered is 'How do I get rid of it?'

This book will answer that question. Ideally, you need to be able to clear a day to get right back on top of things. In fantasy land you'd have several days to sort everything out and start again with a clear desk, but this is the real world, and you have to think fast and act smart. You want:

- **tips for getting on top of things fast**
- **shortcuts for avoiding any unnecessary work**
- **checklists to make sure you have the essentials covered**

… all put together clearly and simply. And short enough to read fast, of course. So here it is.

If time is really pressing (and when isn't it?), you'll find at the back of this book a checklist for getting through the whole process in half a day – maybe an evening when everyone else is off your back. And if you're up to your neck and you can't even find half a day, there's a one-hour version for creating time at the speed of life.

So take a deep breath, and don't panic. Everything you need to know is in this book. This will get your working life back to a manageable state in as little as an hour if that's all you have. You can regard any extra time beyond that as a bonus. So if you have a whole morning, you can already start to feel smug. And if you've had trouble finding the time to read this introduction, then the first section will give you a few tips for making time to read the rest of the book.

You've got the backlog, and the only question you need answered is 'How do I get rid of it?'

work at the speed of life

This book is going to guide you through the six key steps you need to take to clear the backlog of work fast:

1. You'll have to start by creating the time to deal with the pile-up, so we'll begin by doing just that.
2. The next stage is to identify your objective; this means you can tackle the work in the most effective and productive order.
3. After this, we'll establish how to sort all the hundreds (or even thousands) of individual tasks into just a few key groups.
4. The next step involves measuring these groups against your objective so that you can prioritise.
5. Now we come to dealing with the actual tasks themselves, and the options for doing this – do it, defer it, delegate it or dump it.
6. Finally, we'll look at how to handle the tasks you deal with yourself so that they take up as little time as possible.

Throughout the book, we'll also identify ways of preventing the same situation bulding up again in future. So the contents of the book are both a cure for the present and a prevention against future pile-ups.

This book is both a cure for the present and a prevention against future pile-ups

fast thinking gambles

Obviously you're not supposed to get into this state in the first place – but then life was never meant to be this packed. And now you're here, you should ideally give yourself several days to concentrate exclusively on sorting out the piles of paperwork and the mounting voicemail messages. But let's get real. You're doing well to have found the time to read this book and start acting on it.

Just for the record, however, in case you ever find yourself in a parallel existence where work doesn't expand to exceed the time available, why should you allow more time to clear the backlog? Well, there are disadvantages to metaphorically putting a bomb under your desk and wiping out everything on it in a matter of moments.

Without the benefit of a time machine, there are still only 60 minutes to each hour, and 24 hours in a day. There is

doubtless loads of junk on your desk, and plenty of things that are now too late to action, or that should be passed on. But there are still going to be tasks that you need to do, and the more of these there are the longer it will take to do them properly.

- Psychologically, the more time you have to deal with the pile-up, the more manageable and approachable the job seems. The only people who really relish tackling a backlog under time pressure are those irritating creeps who are so damn perfect they never have backlogs in the first place. Do you really want to be like them? (Well yes, actually ... but then, once this lot is cleared, you will be.)
- Of course, following the guidelines in this book you have plenty of time to clear your overload. But knowing that you are doing it under intense time pressure can still be stressful, and does nothing for your relaxation levels or your blood pressure.
- When you come to dealing with those tasks that really do need your attention, it is much less frustrating if you can get them all done easily. When people are out of the office when you call, or suppliers can't get back to you with the figures for at least 48 hours, or your laptop crashes – and all the other everyday irritations that life is peppered with – you are better off having a few days clear ahead of you than needing this all tied up by tomorrow afternoon.
- Some tasks will need to be delegated. However, if these are urgent, you'll hit problems when the person you want to delegate to isn't around. Even if they are around, it can be tough on someone to have an urgent task delegated at

There are disadvantages to metaphorically putting a bomb under your desk and wiping out everything on it

almost no notice – after all, their backlog may be even bigger than yours (there's a refreshing thought).

So, although fast thinking will clear the work effectively, allowing more time for the job will make it even *more* effective and a whole lot less frustrating. Of course, the aim is to follow the tips in this book and avoid ever accumulating another backlog. But if life does catch up with you again, at least try to allow yourself more time to cope with it.

Psychologically, the more time you have to deal with the pile-up, the more manageable and approachable the job seems

1 create the time

So you have six weeks, work to get through in the next two days, and now you've bought this book to help you and it's telling you to find *another* chunk of time to do what it says. Oh great. Just the kind of book you need.

It's a fair cop. It does seem to be missing the point to expect you to find even more time. But deep down, of course, you know that this work isn't going to evaporate by itself. There is simply no option but to take action – and taking action takes time. However, to show that I really am going to help I can start by giving you a few pointers for clearing the time you need.

The MD wants to see you *now*

You might think that you simply can't free up any more time, but I bet you could if a good enough reason came along. How many of the following could you find the time for despite the pile of work on your desk?

- **The MD is finalizing the decision on who to promote, and wants to see you for an hour first thing tomorrow morning.**
- **Your top client calls to say they are almost certain they want to double their last order – but they need you personally to come and meet their MD tomorrow afternoon.**
- **Ditto, and the customer is based on the other side of Europe.**

No doubt you could find the time for most (if not all) of these, however awkward the knock-on effect. OK, so clearing your desk isn't quite as urgent or as important as these, but the point is that it *is* possible to find time if you really need to. You just have to decide that you really need to. Having bought this book, I suspect that you don't need persuading. But in case you do, here's why it's so important to be on top of your work, rather than have your work getting on top of you:

- **If the work piles up, you are likely to miss important or urgent tasks until it is too late to do them properly.**
- **Being overloaded with work is extremely stressful.**
- **If you can't get the routine work out of the way, you can't make time for the important, proactive work.**

There is simply no option but to take action – and taking action takes time

CLEARING A WHOLE DAY

Tell yourself that an essential presentation to a key client or to the board of directors has just been scheduled for all day tomorrow. Can you make it? Great. Now here's some good news. It's just been cancelled. So you can use the whole day that you just freed up to clear your work backlog instead.

- **Successful people are those who get things done. People with piles of work on their desk are not getting things done.**
- **When something important comes along, you cannot give it the attention it deserves without making something else suffer.**

FREEING UP TIME

You know it has got to be done; the only question is how can you make the time for it? Try to clear a whole day if you possibly can, and prevent interruptions:

- **Decide in advance which day you will spend on clearing your desk, and write it in your diary in indelible ink. Do not allow *anything* to displace it. Treat it as you would a diary entry for a vital meeting or the day you fly back from Australia.**
- **Enlist the help of assistants, secretaries or anyone else on your team to support you. Ask them to back up your**

assertion that you are not available to anyone who asks, to field all phone calls and visitors, not to bring you any new work, and not to disturb you all day – just this once.

- You may find that it helps to work some or all of the day from home if you can. Better still, work from somewhere else where no one has a number for you, but you can still make any calls necessary. Maybe you could work from a friend's house (making sure they will be out so they can't bother you, or tempt you with an invitation to the pub for lunch).
- Evenings and weekends are far from ideal, since it is often impossible to delegate at these times, or to action tasks that can be done only during working hours. But you can do the first part of the process – the preparation – out of hours, and arrive at work with a pile of tasks to delegate and another pile of tasks to do yourself (which you still have to allocate time for). This reduces the office time you have to dedicate to clearing the work overload, and can be a good option.

thinking smart

EARLY BIRD

If you absolutely cannot free up this much time at once, how about starting work an hour early each day for a week? This would buy you five hours before anyone else has arrived in the office to pester you. Be strict about forbidding yourself to do anything else in these five hours other than clear the pile-up of work.

You are clearly pretty committed by now to sorting out your workload, so you will find the time simply because you must. The longer you leave it, the worse it will get (which is what my mother used to say to me about tidying my bedroom, which is the same thing really; much as it galls me to say it, she was right). So the three key steps are:

- **Pick your time.**
- **Stick to it.**
- **Eliminate distractions and interruptions.**

Simple as that, really.

The longer you leave it, the worse it will get

2 your objective

You may not have been expecting this one. In fact, you might wonder where setting objectives comes into the whole thing of offloading as much work as possible. But, in fact, it is central to the exercise. I'm not talking about the objective of this particular process – which we know is to turn the mountain of work on your desk, your computer, your voicemail and your mental list into something smaller than a molehill. I'm talking about the big stuff. Your personal objective. What are you here for?

You may have only a few hours to clear the backlog, but you still need to dedicate the first five minutes to this. It is easy to forget, among the weekly meetings, budgets, requests for information, invoices for approval and all the rest of it, that your core function is something else: to increase sales, raise customer satisfaction, boost PR, improve productivity, or whatever it is the company is really paying you to do.

thinking fast

TAKING TIME TO MAKE TIME

Identifying your objective doesn't have to take long – five minutes at the most and probably less. But the whole process of clearing the work overload will be much faster in the long run if you just give this the time it needs.

Of course all the other things are important, and I'm not suggesting they shouldn't be done. But if you are not achiving your core objective, all the rest is worthless. So identify a clear objective. Here are some possible examples:

- **sales: increase profits**
- **accounts: ensure accurate, helpful billing and payment systems**
- **production: improve productivity**
- **PR: increase positive public awareness**
- **distribution: ensure fast, high-quality distribution at minimum cost**
- **marketing: build customer loyalty and attract new customers.**

You may work in one of these areas and feel the main thrust of your job is slightly different – that's fine. These are only examples. For instance, as a marketing

If you are not achieving your core objective, all the rest is worthless

WHAT WILL YOU LEAVE BEHIND?

If you're not entirely clear what your objective should be, try asking yourself this question: when you move on from this job, what single aspect of your company's performance do you hope to have improved? Customer satisfaction? Sales figures? Productivity? Costs? Public awareness? The answer to this will tell you what your objective is.

executive you might be employed primarily to focus on attracting new customers, while your sales team is charged with building loyalty.

If you really haven't a clue what your objective is, there is something amiss in your organization and I suspect that you are not the only one with a work overload. Your job description ought to be clear on the subject, or failing that your boss should be able to give you a straight answer.

You need this objective to be clear, because you cannot prioritize your workload without it, as we'll see later. Clearly, work that directly helps you achieve your objective is more important than all the other mountains of work that don't. And you cannot identify which tasks belong in this category until you know your objective. So, however rushed you are, this is an essential step.

for next time

Once you have cleared the overload, your objective remains important for helping you prioritize in future. But that's not all. The smart way to work is to block in time in your diary every week which is dedicated directly to achieving your objective. Aim for a couple of half days a week, and during these times do only work that will further that objective. Include time for coming up with new ideas too.

It is the people who manage to do this who really make successes of their jobs. They don't simply keep things ticking over; they actively make things happen. They are the ones who are noticed by top management, and who rise up the ladder fastest. So, if you're not already one of them, now's the time to start.

You need this objective to be clear, because you cannot prioritize your workload without it

3 organizing the tasks

I know, I know, you just want to get on and *do* the work, not mess about organizing it first. But trust me; this really will help in the long run. Not only will you get through the pile of work faster, you will also do the work better. Honest.

There are two reasons for this stage:

- **Psychologically, a lot of the problem with tackling a work overload is that your mind sees a huge nebulous collection of tasks – some written down, some stored on computer or voicemail, some running loose in your head – and it all seems impossible to cope with. But once you organize it, you have taken control of it, and you have reduced it to a form that your mind can comprehend. This somehow makes the whole job seem manageable, and gives you a huge positive boost.**
- **Once you have sorted out the work logically, you will be able to do it more efficiently. If you approach it haphazardly, you will keep losing your thread, and you will miss opportunities to streamline tasks. You might**

find, for example, that one of the pieces of paperwork on your desk postdates another, and makes it redundant. But if you get to the redundant one first you'll act on it anyway, and then find later that you wasted your time. So organizing the work will speed things up later on.

So how are you going to organize it? Start by getting everything down on paper – yes, paper; forget about computer screens because you need to move things around physically. Write down any tasks that currently exist only in your head. Write each on a fresh piece of paper, because they may end up in different piles. Print out any notes, e-mails or anything else that needs action. You will also need to write down any key diary dates in the next few days, especially those that clash.

thinking smart

MAKE ROOM

Clear physical space for this part of the process, so that you have plenty of room. If the work looks visually organized, your mind will be more organized. If you are working among a mass of papers and files on your desk, you will continue to feel disorganized mentally. So find a clear table, or even the floor, to amass your piles of paper on.

Organizing the work will speed things up later on

Sorting into groups

Now you need to start sorting out piles of paper. Don't worry – it won't take long. This is the point where you should start to relax because you are getting on with something: creating order out of chaos. So what are these piles of paper? Well, that depends on your work. You need to create one pile for each key job you have in hand. You'll probably find that at least some of the paperwork is already sorted – you may already have half a pile of notes and papers to do with next week's presentation which you haven't started on yet, and a file bulging with data for your budget which you're supposed to have drawn up.

These are the kinds of categories you are sorting everything into. You should create a pile for each major project or task:

- **a pile of applications, job description and so on for a post you are trying to fill**
- **a bundle of papers and post-it notes for next month's exhibition**
- **a pile of letters to sign**
- **a file of data to go into a report you are writing**
- **a collection of phone calls you should be returning**
- **all the stuff to be filed**
- **a pile of reading material**

… and so on. You'll have to decide what the exact groups are, but that's the general idea.

SORTING THE LEFTOVERS

It may have occurred to you that you will probably have some items that don't fit into groups – they are one-off tasks, or perhaps just a couple of related tasks that don't really constitute a group. Or, of course, they may be rubbish: out-of-date figures, e-mails that have been superseded, and notes to call colleagues who left the company over a year ago (I'm sure your backlog doesn't really go back that far). So you need another two piles:

- *Miscellaneous*: This is where you put everything that doesn't go anywhere else. However, this becomes in effect a pile of everything that hasn't

thinking fast

MORE RATHER THAN LESS

At this stage, you should go for more groups rather than fewer if you're in doubt. Maybe you are advertising two posts at the moment. Should all the stuff go in one pile or two? If you feel strongly about it, do what feels right. But if you're not sure, split it into two for now. Don't waste time agonizing over it. (You can always combine them later if you change your mind.)

been sorted properly, which isn't a particularly good thing. So try to keep it as small as possible. If it starts to expand, you may find that you can create fresh groups from it. Suppose you had put in this pile a reminder to deal with a member of your team whose timekeeping is poor, and an email from a colleague asking you to allocate three people to help staff the exhibition stand next week, and a request from one of your team members to move to another desk further from the coffee machine where there are fewer distractions. These could form the basis of a group of tasks related to personnel matters.

2 *Rubbish*: Feel free to throw anything away that you can. Bear in mind, though, that there will be another opportunity to throw things away later, so don't spend ages dithering about it here. If you're sure you can chuck it – great. But don't waste time thinking about it. Better to get on and organize your groups fairly fast for now.

At the end of this process you should have, apart from your miscellaneous and rubbish piles, about half a dozen to a dozen key groups, and a few smaller ones. You've probably spent somewhere in the region of half an hour or so getting to this stage. And you should be starting to feel a whole lot better already.

thinking smart

POSITIVE PILE-UP

You can put your rubbish straight in the bin if you like. But if there's a lot of it, you may find it hugely encouraging to keep a pile for it so that you can see how much progress you're making. This is just the sort of positive boost that can make the whole operation more satisfying. And that, in turn, can help you to work through it faster.

KEEPING NOTES

If ever you find yourself with a serious overload again (as if!), it would be great to have a backlog that wasn't full of post-it notes and scraps of paper. The way around this is simple: carry a notebook with you and write down all your notes in it. These

thinking smart

Don't assume that everyone else maintains your high standard of organization. If someone says they'll call you back, make a note so that if they let you down you're still on the case. Otherwise it goes out of your head until, for example, two minutes before the meeting at which you need the information they were going to give you. The same goes for suppliers getting back to you with quotes and so on. Every week, when you clear your miscellaneous file, you'll catch up with these.

You've probably spent somewhere in the region of half an hour or so getting to this stage

notes should include all those loose ideas and thoughts in your head – get them down on paper instead. If other people pass you post-its, you can stick them in the notebook.

As long as you don't leave the notebook on the train, you have everything in one place. And because it's portable, you have it with you all the time, so as a bonus you can take advantage of any spare five minutes when you're away from the office to catch up on some of the items in it.

for next time

It is more efficient to work on one project at a time, rather than to jump from one thing to another and back again. So, ideally, you need to keep a file for each project or logical group of tasks from the start. Each email or post-it note or piece of paper goes into the correct file from the offset. You can have a miscellaneous file too (commonly known as an in-tray), but allocate a certain amount of time each week to clearing it. How about doing it at 4.30 on a Friday afternoon, and you can go home as soon as the file is empty? It shouldn't take long.

fast thinking pause

HAVE A BREAK

Break, we're getting there.

Notes should include all those loose ideas and thoughts in your head

4 prioritizing

No, I'm sorry, it still isn't time to get on with your tasks. First, you have to know which ones to get on with. You're up against the clock, and you can't clear all the work instantly. Some will be scheduled for later. So you want to be sure that the work is tackled in the right order, the most important tasks are given the time they deserve, and nothing urgent is left till last. There are two aspects of prioritizing to address:

- **importance**
- **urgency.**

Importance

This is where your objective is so useful. Simply take each group in turn and measure it against your original objective – increasing profits, raising customer satisfaction or whatever it is. Will this task help you directly to achieve your objective? Mark each group of tasks A, B or C, where A means that the task is central to your objective, and C means it is of little direct relevance.

Suppose you are an accounts manager: here are three groups of tasks to set against your objective – to ensure accurate, helpful billing and payment systems. You should be able to see which directly further it and which don't.

Remember: we are not concerned with urgency at the moment – that comes later. We are simply establishing importance at the moment. The presentation, for example, may not need preparing for a fortnight, but when the time comes it will be crucial.

A few people have more than one objective in their job. This is less common than you might think, because your objective is fairly broad and is

Group of tasks	Objective	Importance to objective
Prepare a presentation to persuade the board to invest in new invoicing software	Ensure accurate, helpful billing and payment systems	A
Plan move into larger office	Ensure accurate, helpful billing and payment systems	C
Plan selection of new accounts supervisor	Ensure accurate, helpful billing and payment systems	B

generally very close to the objective of the department. Don't be tempted to think you have more than one objective when in fact both are part of the same overall objective. But perhaps your job spans two departments. Perhaps you work for both sales and marketing.

In this case, any task that is vital to meeting *either* objective is an A-grade task. So you can prioritize in just the same way as you would with only one objective.

You should be starting to see how you were actually saving yourself time when you were sorting all those pieces of paperwork into groups. Instead of having to establish the importance of hundreds of tasks, you have only to deal with a dozen or so categories. All the tasks within each category fall into the same level of importance.

thinking smart

WHAT IF ...?

If you have trouble working out the importance of any group of tasks, try asking yourself what would happen if you simply didn't do it. What would be the effect on the organization? If it would mean a cut in profits, mounting costs or damaging PR for example, award it a grade A. If it would make little significant difference in the long term, give it a C.

URGENCY

Urgent tasks are, obviously, those that must be done as soon as possible. When you prioritize you have to identify urgency separately from importance, otherwise you will become muddled. Some tasks merit only a C when measured against your objective, and yet you know you need to give them your attention, and soon.

So identify urgent groups of tasks as a separate issue. Arranging the move to a bigger office, for example, may be urgent even though it scored only a C. These urgent groups will be fed into the overall priority list, as we'll see in just a moment. However, they should not be allocated too much time (unless they are also important). These are the tasks to get out of the way first, that's all.

What if you have tasks on your list which you don't consider urgent but someone else does? For example, one of your colleagues can't finalize the details for the press launch until you decide the date of it. It's still a few weeks away and you're in no hurry, but your colleague is getting very edgy.

If the task is really quick, it's probably better just to list it as urgent and keep everyone happy. But it could be a long job. What then? In that case, be objective. Does your colleague have a valid point? How important is the press launch? How much

identify urgency separately from importance

does the precise date matter? Decide whether the task itself is urgent, not whether it is urgent to you or to somebody else.

Your priorities

You should now be able to put all your groups of tasks into order of priority. The first ones to tackle are the really urgent ones, even if they are not that important. (If they are both urgent and important, then they come right at the top of the list, of course.) Then come the remaining tasks in order of importance:

1 urgent and important

2 urgent

3 important (A)

4 important (B)

5 important (C).

Even the least important tasks will be dealt with in time, because they will eventually become urgent and thereby jump to the top of the list – that's if you haven't got round to doing them first (and if pigs have learnt to fly).

thinking smart

WORD OF WARNING

It is very tempting to move the tasks you enjoy up your list, and put the tasks you don't want to do at the bottom of the list. Don't do it. Be brutally objective about ranking tasks, or you will end up back where you started before you know it – with unimportant jobs done and a pile of taks on your desk which are urgent and important and should have been done already. You've got to deal with it all sooner or later, so when it comes to your least favourite tasks, just bite the bullet.

You presumably decided to read this book because you had a huge pile of things to do and you wanted to get rid of the backlog and make a fresh start with a clear desk. This book seemed to suggest, improbably, that you could do all these myriad tasks in as little as an hour if you only knew how.

But in fact – as may be becoming apparent – you don't have to *do* all of them now at all. You only have to do a few now, and either offload or defer the rest. The real exercise is in deciding which to tackle now, and how to handle the rest in a realistic timescale. There's a relief!

The real exercise is about which tasks to tackle now, and how to handle the rest later

COLOUR CODING

Why not use three different colours of files for all your work, coded according to importance? This means you are constantly reminding yourself of where your priorities really lie, and it saves a lot of time whenever you come to prioritize your workload (even when it isn't piling up).

for next time

If you want to prevent overloads in future, one of the ways is to prioritise tasks as you go. Whenever a new project arises, or you start a new file, ascribe it a level of importance – A, B or C – by measuring it against your objective.

Each week, preferably on Monday morning, prioritise all your current files for the week. Not only will this remind you of which tasks are the key ones to focus on – perhaps that presentation is your main focus for this week – but it also means that the system will pick up any low-importance tasks that are becoming urgent.

When you schedule time for urgent tasks that are not important, don't allow more time than you have to. These are not tasks to hang around over – they need to be got out of the way as quickly as possible to make way for the important work.

Each week, preferably on Monday morning, prioritise all your current files for the week

5 the options

Now you know what order you need to work through your groups in, it is finally time to start doing it. Well, almost. First, you need to go through the tasks in each group and sort them into four categories. The point of this is to identify the tasks that you absolutely have to deal with now, and find an alternative way of coping with all the rest of them. This is where you really start to slim down your immediate workload so that it becomes manageable. This is time well spent, however little you have.

There are only four things you can do with each task:

- **dump it**
- **delegate it**
- **defer it**
- **do it.**

WHICH OPTION TO CHOOSE?

As you go through each of your groups, you can sort everything in it into one of these four categories. We'll look at delegating and deferring in more detail later in this chapter, and in the next chapter at doing the tasks you can't sensibly offload. But here is what you need to know to sort the groups:

Dump it. You've already had one quick dumping session, but now's the time to be brutal. Look, you've got a huge overload of work here, and you simply can't afford to be dealing with things that you don't need to, or even finding space for them on your desk. So, if in doubt, just dump it. Suppose you dump fifty things, ten of which you're not quite sure about. What are the odds on regretting it? Maybe one of the ten will rebound – so what? You can always ask for another copy of an invoice, or look up a phone number you thought you'd finished with. Better just to dump the lot now and take the minor consequences later. They probably won't happen at all.

Delegate it. Delegating is a skilled task (don't worry, you'll have learnt it by the end of this chapter). For the moment, you just need to know which tasks to delegate – we'll look at how to delegate them later. And the answer is very easy – does it have to be you who does this task? If not, pass it on to someone else, whether it is urgent or not. There's just one proviso: some tasks take

Identify the tasks that you absolutely have to deal with now, and find an alternative way of coping with all the rest of them

11 thinking smart

SAVE IT FOR LATER

Don't be tempted to address the most important tasks now simply because they are important. If they are not urgent, they can still be deferred. It will give you more time to do them justice.

longer to explain than to do yourself. With proper delegation (as we'll see), this isn't generally an issue, but when you're racing to clear your desk as fast as possible, a few quick tasks might be better off in your 'do it' pile than in your 'delegate it' pile.

Defer it. Again, we'll look at how to handle these tasks later. But essentially, if a job needs to be done by you but it isn't urgent, you can do it later. Pretty obvious really. The only thing is that there's no point deferring ten days' work to be done by the end of next week, on to the top of next week's workload, or you'll find yourself going through exactly this process again next Friday.

Do it. Everything that can't be dumped, delegated or deferred will have to be done. However, by the time you've reached the end of this sort-out, your 'do it' pile should be looking refreshingly small compared to the mountain you started out with an hour or so ago.

Schedule your time

You'll need to do a quick sort-through of all your groups – or at least all but the very low-priority ones – before you go any further. In theory, you might think that you could do each group as you get to it. However, it is very hard to plan your time if you do this. Suppose you have four hours left to clear this backlog. How long can you spend on the first group? That rather depends on how much else you have to fit into the time, doesn't it? And that is determined by how many of the tasks in the other groups you are going to have to do today. So you'll have to do a basic sort-through of your key groups so that you can allocate your time appropriately.

Once you have been through your groups, and can see which contain the most time-consuming tasks that you are going to have to do now, plan out your time before you begin. Take into account both the estimated amount of work in the group and its importance. Work through the groups in order of the priority you have established. That way, if anything goes horribly wrong and your time is cut short, at least the most crucial tasks will have been done.

GIVE IT TIME

The earlier in the process you identify urgent tasks that you can delegate, the earlier you can set them in motion. It's no good giving someone a pile of tasks at 4.30 in the afternoon and asking them to have them done by 5.30. Better to have handed them over straight after lunch. And if you don't find the task until 8.30 in the evening, it will be almost impossible to delegate it for completion before tomorrow morning. You'll end up having to do it yourself. So identify early on those urgent tasks that you can delegate, and get the ball rolling.

Here are a few guidelines to help you set a schedule after you've sorted everything into the four categories:

1 Do all your urgent delegating first (following the delegating principles we'll be looking at in a moment).
2 Separate out the tasks you can delegate later when your poor minions have got over the shock of the pile of work you've just given them.
3 Schedule your most urgent tasks next, but unless they are also important don't spend much time on them.

4 You may find you need to do one or two urgent tasks from a group first, before you get to the rest of the group. This is fine – tackle whole groups at a time otherwise, but obviously urgent tasks must be handled first. Maybe the pile relating to Friday's presentation can wait, but you may need to phone your supplier to talk about prices urgently to give them time to work out costs and get back to you later.

5 Look at the number of groups to deal with, and the amount of time, and schedule according to the average time per group. So, if you have four hours and eight groups, you should average half an hour per group.

6 Now you can do a few quick trade-offs. Suppose you want more time to work on next week's exhibition – up its allocation to an hour, and give two minor groups fifteen minutes each instead. Keep trading off like this until you are happy with the balance. This should be a quick process, but then I doubt you'll feel inclined to spend all afternoon on it.

7 Whatever schedule you draw up, *stick to it*. If you get ahead, that's fine. But don't let yourself slip behind. Keep checking the clock to make sure you are on course.

Scheduling will ensure you don't reach the end of your time before you reach the end of the workload

INVESTING NOT WASTING

Drawing up schedules may not seem like a clever use of time. You are doubtless itching to get on with all those piles of tasks by now. But it is the only way to make sure you don't reach the end of your time before you reach the end of the workload. One of the first things we tend to do when we are rushing is to stop thinking. But by thinking *smart* – setting an objective, drawing up a schedule and so on – we are investing a few minutes now to save a load of time later. Trust me.

Scheduling your time may look like a huge job, but it isn't really. It should take you five minutes at the most, and you'll have a game plan to last you the rest of the day (or evening, or whatever it is you have).

for next time

Learn to recognize the tasks, e-mails and post-it notes that will end up being dumped, and don't keep them in the first place. Delete e-mail messages after you've opened them whenever you can – without printing them out. Reassure yourself with the thought that you can always get them back if you have to. Just don't send them to the recycle bin. If you have a note with a phone number on, either bin it or enter it in your phone book, but don't keep it lying around.

Equally, delegate what you can even when you think you aren't overloaded. There are always more important things to free up time for – planning, developing ideas and so on. The earlier you delegate a task, the fairer you are being on the person you delegate it to, and the better chance they have of doing it well.

6 delegating

If you have staff you are authorized to delegate to, and you have a work overload, you are almost certainly not delegating as effectively as you could. In fact, delegation is a core management skill and the mark of a good team leader. Once you have learnt to delegate well, you are much less likely to build up a work overload in the first place (or at least it will happen a lot less often). The pace of the modern business world is so fast that unless you delegate whatever you can you are bound to be swamped quickly by your workload.

UNDERSTANDING DELEGATION

Delegation is often misunderstood. It is not just a case of offloading simple tasks which you haven't time for yourself (or don't enjoy). That is simply allocation of tasks and has no long-term value. Delegation, on the other hand, not only creates more time for you to get on with the important job of managing your team, but it also helps to develop your team members' skills, to make the team as a whole more effective – to your credit and theirs.

thinking smart

PASS IT ON

Don't assume, simply because your boss has delegated a task to you, that you can't delegate it yourself. After all, you are still accountable for it and taking overall responsibility. So long as your boss gets the same result, what does it matter who performs the task?

So, the whole business of delegating means delegating responsibility for tasks. Give your team member a target, with specified time, cost and quality constraints, and let them decide how to achieve it. That way they learn more, they get the boost of achieving a positive result, and they take some of your workload from you. You retain overall accountability, of course. If anything goes wrong, you carry the can – but then half the skill is in delegating well so that nothing does go wrong, as we'll see.

Many people fear that by delegating part of their workload they will lose control. But think about what you lose control of: the details and minutiae that occupy too much of your time; the phone calls and research and e-mails and paperwork. You are still in overall control of the tasks you delegate. And you have made time to stand back and look at the big picture. You can see opportunities to grasp, spot threats in

Delegating creates more time for you to get on with the important job of managing your team

11 thinking smart

WHEN YOU'RE NOT THERE...

Ask yourself this question: 'If I were away ill or on business for a month, which tasks simply couldn't be done?' There should be almost none. Everything else not on this list can be delegated.

time to stave them off, and develop ideas to boost your team's achievements and impress your boss.

DELEGATION SKILLS

When you're clearing the backlog and you're up against the clock, you may well end up delegating the odd boring but necessary task just to get it done fast. But not everything on your desk is urgent, and you should be able to apply the principles of delegation properly to most of them. So here are the key steps to delegating successfully:

1 Review the task and set the objective. Here we go, setting objectives again. Have you noticed how setting the objective is the first step in almost all management skills? That's because if you don't know where you're going, your chances of arriving there are seriously hampered. An objective is a destination: once you know it you can plan your route, estimate the time you will take, identify whether any alternatives or shortcuts will be helpful or not, and know when you have reached the end of the journey.

So start by identifying the task and setting an objective for it. Bundle together groups of tasks with the same objective. So if you need some research done for your proposal, get one person to do it all – costings, performance data, packaging options, competitor comparisons and all the rest. The objective is to find the data that will support your proposal and make it more convincing.

2 Decide who to delegate it to. Not every task suits every person. When time is not an issue, try to stretch people with the tasks you delegate to them. They will find it more rewarding. Even crucial tasks can go to someone skilled and capable but without experience of that particular task. That way you are continuously building the experience and capability of your whole team.

At the same time, there's no point giving someone a task that simply doesn't suit them and wastes their talents. If you want someone to do your research, find someone who is quite methodical and good with people if they need to coax information about competitors out of suppliers, or to persuade someone busy to spend

An objective is a destination: once you know it you can plan your route

WHEN YOU'RE PUSHED FOR TIME, GO FOR EXPERIENCE

If you're in a hurry, it's a good idea to delegate to someone who will already know how to do the task with relatively little support from you. When you have time, however, try finding someone who will be more stretched by it, and who will learn from it. Once you've trained them up, they will be encouraged and you will have one more skilled person to delegate to next time.

time tracking down data. Don't delegate the tasks to a brash ideas person who is great at getting things started but then wants to move straight on to the next task without seeing the thing through.

3 Set parameters. You're giving the person you delegate this task to an objective. They need to know what they are supposed to achieve and why. But they will need more than just this. They will want to know how long they've got, what authority they have (to ask for input from other people, for example) and so on. So you need to provide:

- **objective**
- **deadline**
- **quality standards**

- **budget**
- **limits of authority**
- **details of any resources available.**

You are not, however, telling them how to do the job. You are telling them everything they need to give you the results you want – including when you want them, at what cost and so on. But how they get there is up to them. To return to the analogy of the objective as a destination, they are free to plan their own route so long as they arrive on time, having consumed an acceptable amount of fuel and not crashed the car. By all means ask them to outline their route to you, but don't make them change it to suit you. If you can see a problem they haven't anticipated, point it out and let *them* find the solution.

4 Check they understand. Encourage them to talk to you about the task, so you can make sure they understand exactly what is required and why. You can suggest ideas, so long as you are not railroading them into adopting your approach.

5 Give them back-up. Help all you can. Clear the way with another department head for them to get support from their team; tell them where to find information that you know about and they don't; give them access to any useful documents;

If you can see a problem, point it out and let *them* find the solution

DOUBLING UP

If the task is a major project, or even if it is relatively small but time is tight, you can always delegate it to more than one person. Generally, the best approach is to appoint a task leader, and brief everyone at the same time so they all know what's needed.

let them have a draft copy of the proposal that their research will go into (I take it you generally write a draft well in advance?)

6 Monitor their progress. Schedule feedback sessions for a major, long-term project. Even for a brief task, check how it's going – frequent, informal feedback often works better than a formal session. This gives them a chance to check with you that they are on course, that they aren't wasting their time on too much detail, or missing a key angle. It boosts their confidence in the job they are doing, and reassures you that everything is on track.

Monitoring, however, does not mean interfering. Look out for any sign that they have made an error and not noticed it, but don't fuss about trivial mistakes. These are almost inevitable, and you'd probably have made equivalent mistakes if you'd done

thinking smart

KEEPING TABS

Just because you're up against the clock, it doesn't mean you can't monitor progress. After all, you still need to be sure that the task gets done properly. If you've delegated an urgent task to be done by the end of the day, you can still call or pop your head round the door half way through the afternoon to check that it's going OK.

the task yourself. You should intervene only if serious mistakes threaten, and then only for as long as it takes to get the job back on course. Taking a task away from someone is deeply demoralizing and should be done only in extreme circumstances. If you delegate well from the start it should never be necessary.

7 Evaluate their performance. After the task is completed, sit down with the team member involved and evaluate what they have done. Give praise and recognition where it is deserved, and even if the results were disappointing find aspects of their performance to praise. Make sure that they – and you – have learnt any lessons you need to from the exercise. And remember that the ultimate responsibility for failure, as well as for success, lies with you.

You should intervene only if serious mistakes threaten

Those are the basic principles of delegation, so now do it, at least as far as you can under your current time constraints. Before you move on to deal with the rest of your workload, go and delegate anything that is really urgent and has to be done in the next 24 hours.

Now set aside all the rest of your work to delegate (still grouped in order of priority), so that you can delegate it later and give it the time to think it through properly according to the principles we've just looked at. There. That should be quite a large chunk of your backlog taken care of.

So don't view delegation as a way of offloading jobs you don't like or don't have time for. It is actually a key opportunity for you to exercise your skill as a manager in developing your team.

thinking smart

GET AHEAD

If you delegate work well in advance of when you need it completed, you can set a deadline that gives you plenty of leeway for building it into a subsequent project of your own. So, for example, you can get the research for your proposal completed and delivered to you ten days before you have to write the thing – giving you plenty of time to incorporate it into your own work.

for next time

Identify tasks for delegating as soon as they arrive on your desk, or as soon as you generate the work. This gives the maximum time to get ahead of yourself, and for the person to whom you delegate the work to get it done.

The aim is to build the skills of your whole team continuously, so always think hard about the best person to delegate each task to. Up against the clock, you just want to give the job to someone you know who can be left alone to get on with it. But, in the long term, this doesn't stretch or challenge anyone. The better you are at delegating, the better your team will become at performing delegated tasks, and the easier it will be for you to delegate future tasks. And your team members will feel motivated, confident and appreciated, which can only benefit their performance.

Delegating is a key opportunity for you to exercise your skill as a manager

7 deferring tasks

Deferring might seem, at first glance, to be a bad idea. After all, it's just another word for putting things off, isn't it? And isn't that why you got into this mess in the first place? Too much work and too little time, so you've been putting things off until there's such a backlog that you can't find your desk under the heap of papers and notes.

Well, yes and no. Deferring is a sort of structured, organized putting things off, which makes a big difference. It means putting things off until there's time to do them – and making that time if necessary – rather than simply putting them off and then *not* doing them.

Let's just recap where we've got to, so you can see how much you've achieved already:

- You've found time to read this book, and at least a few more hours for actually doing the job – clearing your work overload.
- You've identified your core objective.
- You've got all your tasks down on paper, and organized them into groups.
- You've set the groups in order of priority according to both urgency and importance, by measuring them against your objective.
- You've sorted the contents of each group into four categories: tasks to dump, delegate, defer or do.
- You've scheduled your remaining time (check now to see how you're doing).
- You're dumping everything you can as you work through each group.
- You're also delegating whatever you don't need to do yourself – or setting it aside to delegate later if it isn't urgent.

You should by now be looking at a much smaller pile of work; and instead of being chaotic, it should now be neatly ordered. I hope you're starting to feel smug. All the remaining tasks as you sort through each group are ones that you need to do yourself – no more dumping or passing on. However, you still have two categories remaining: tasks to defer and tasks to do today. We'll start by

Deferring tasks isn't about putting them in a pending pile: it's about allocating a specific time to do them

finding out how to defer tasks effectively, and the next chapter will tackle tasks you have to do now.

Deferring tasks isn't about putting them in a pending pile: it's about allocating a specific time to do them. When life travels at the rate of an express train, almost any task that isn't scheduled will end up cluttering up your desk or your brain until an impending deadline impels you into last-minute action. So the answer is to schedule everything. Yes, everything.

In the long term, the key to keeping on top of the workload is to put everything in your diary, so we'll look at that in a moment. But right now, you're probably not interested in the long term. You just want to finish clearing this pile of work.

So look at the groups you have left. Look at your diary for the next couple of weeks. Now schedule in the tasks in order of priority, blocking out time in your diary. So you might block out half a day to plan your proposal, and another day the following week to write it. You might schedule a couple of hours to catch up on non-urgent phone calls. Perhaps you need to block in time to plan your budget or hold appraisals. And, of course, you'll need some time to delegate all the tasks in your non-urgent delegation pile.

I've already suggested allocating the last hour of a Friday afternoon to deal with miscellaneous tasks (if you had time to read that bit). So

SCHEDULE THE SCHEDULE

If you're really short of time now, just schedule in one block of time in the next couple of days to spend on planning your diary. That way, you can defer not only the tasks but the scheduling of them as well. You presumably don't need me to tell you that if you don't do your scheduling at the time you've allocated, you'll just end up back here again all too soon.

remember you can allow time for general tasks such as correspondence as well as for major projects. You will still need to keep your objective in mind here, and be sure you give each group of tasks the time it deserves. Schedule everything – even if it needs only five minutes – otherwise it's not going to get done.

You need to make sure of two things to make this deferring business work.

1 **Be realistic.** There's no point scheduling time that it isn't possible to find. You'll just be demoralized, the work won't get done, and instead of being overworked you'll be overworked *and* miserable. So, reckon to work as fast and as smart as you can, but don't expect yourself to work miracles, creating 30 hours in every day, or waving

Deferring tasks isn't about putting them in a pending pile, it's about allocating a specific time to do them

a wand so that your boss's interminable Monday morning meeting lasts only ten minutes. If you know it never finishes before 11 a.m., don't schedule anything else before then (unless you can get away with doing it during the meeting).

2 **Be firm.** If you don't adhere to the schedule you have set yourself, then the whole exercise will be a waste of time. Once you start to slip, you will become demotivated and slip further. So be really strict with yourself. If your working life is punctuated regularly with emergency calls that may have to interrupt your scheduled tasks, allow for this. Build catching-up time into your schedule.

thinking smart

DON'T GO HOME

Make a rule that you won't go home until you have completed that day's tasks. So if you don't stick to your schedule, you pay for it in the evening. You'll soon learn to schedule realistically, and in the meantime the work will still get done. The idea is not to keep staying late, but to make sure you never need to.

thinking smart

CANCEL WHAT YOU CAN

Regular meetings eat into your time in a big way. What's more, they can end up occupying a part of almost every day, so that you can never free up a whole day without several weeks' notice. So, see if you can reduce the number of regular meetings. For example:

- Could you make your weekly meetings fortnightly or even monthly?
- Could a conference call replace some meetings and occupy less time?
- Could fewer people attend? (This always speeds things up.)
- Can you excuse yourself from other people's regular meetings?

thinking smart

EARLY BIRD

It's a good idea to give yourself half an hour at the start of each day for planning the day's workload and dealing with any quick but urgent tasks – signing a couple of letters, returning a phone call from yesterday, checking a team member is coping with a task you delegated, answering urgent correspondence and so on. So if you start work at, say, 9 a.m., don't schedule any appointments before 9.30. This works better than leaving time at the end of the day, which often tends to be taken over by the afternoon's activities.

If you don't adhere to the schedule you have set yourself, then the whole exercise will be a waste of time

And how do you know exactly what you have to do? Most of it should be in your diary already. Planning your diary means turning it from an occasional reference book into an indispensible interactive guide. Your diary should be a key tool for doing your job, and you should be making regular notes in it. Have a big desk diary if you can't write small enough for a pocket one. Every time someone says 'Call me next Tuesday,' down it should go in your diary entry for next Tuesday. Not on a post-it note that could get lost. And add a phone number if you have it to hand, to save looking it up again next week. So your to-do list should be half-written before you ever get there.

You should also note down in your diary when you are expecting call-backs, e-mails or answers from other people. Otherwise, if you leave the ball in their court and they let you down, the task is under no one's control. So, whenever someone says 'I'll get back to you by the end of the week,' make a note in the diary for Friday to check they have done so.

You can prioritize the tasks on your to-do list so that you do the most urgent ones first. Then, if a crisis happens, you've only got to delay the less urgent tasks. If they are of equal urgency, do the most important first (back to your objective again). You can prioritize in any way that suits you. For example:

- mark the highest-priority tasks A, the next batch B, and the lowest-priority tasks C (three categories should be plenty);
- colour-code tasks according to priority using highlighter pens (again, three colours should do fine);
- list the tasks in order of priority so you simply work your way down the list.

So, deferring tasks isn't the same thing as putting them off. It is the way to create time so that all your tasks get done efficiently and at the best time. And you never again have to deal with a work overload like this one.

thinking smart

WORKING JOURNEY

Why not plan your day on the way to work? If you travel by train or are driven, you can write out your to-do list and your phone calls as you go. If you drive yourself, you can think it through in your head – or talk it into a dictaphone – and simply jot it all down when you arrive.

Planning ensures that you can spend time on the things that really matter

for next time

Diary planning is a crucial skill for staying on top of the work and – just as importantly – for making sure that you invest the bulk of your time in the really important tasks: those that further your core objective.

As soon as you get the chance (and you can schedule this in your diary now), you should take time to plan your diary for the rest of the year. No, that's not a printing error – I meant year. You should sit down once a year and plan key dates into your diary. Obviously you can't schedule everything that far in advance, so you'll also need to have a planning session at the start of each month. Then there's the weekly diary session too, and your daily planning, of course.

You may be thinking that you bought this book to pick up some fast tips on how to clear a hectic backlog of work. And suddenly you're being lectured to by some time-obsessed, crazed lunatic with a fascist desire to plan every last second of your day to the point where there's no time left to do any of the actual work.

But actually, this is a perfectly normal, sane approach to organizing your time (of course, I would say that). No, really. The point is that once you've got into the swing of planning it takes very little time. But it ensures that you are in control of your time and your actions. In particular, it ensures that you can spend time on the things that really matter; tasks that help you achieve your objective.

By the end of the planning process, every single task should have time scheduled for it. It may simply be part of 'miscellaneous' or 'correspondence', but there will be a window of time set aside for dealing with it. If there isn't, it won't get done. So let's go through the whole process.

YEARLY PLANNING

At the start of the year, spend half an hour or so entering in all the dates you already know about for the rest of the year:

- regular meetings
- special events (exhibitions or conferences, for example)
- regular events (such as a weekly pub lunch with the team, or an hour on a Friday afternoon to deal with miscellaneous tasks)
- holidays
- personal time (days you want to leave early for the kids' birthdays or your best friend's wedding).

You'll also need to set aside about fifteen minutes diary-planning time at the start of each month. Then also set aside whole days throughout the year for working on proactive tasks that will really produce results. This is when you will develop ideas and plan new projects geared to boosting your company's performance. This might be a strategic planning session with your team, preparing your annual budget, or working on a proposal for a new system to improve your department's productivity. This is what you are here for and this time is essential for the organization, and for you to shine in your own career. Start by setting aside at least a full day a month, but increase this if you feel you can.

Do not be tempted to cancel time allocated for key tasks

Obviously, throughout the year, you will add in key meetings, customer appointments, presentations and so on, as dates are set for them.

MONTHLY PLANNING

This is your chance to schedule in all your key tasks for the month which you didn't know about when you did your yearly planning. In fact, we're talking about the type of tasks you are currently trying to schedule in. If you plan them at the start of the month, it's much easier to fit them all in with time to spare for routine tasks and things that crop up later. These might include:

- selection or appraisal interviews
- visits to customers or suppliers
- presentations, including preparation time
- time to prepare for reports and proposals
- time to delegate key tasks.

Your monthly planning sessions have another function too. They give you a chance to review your workload over the month. Not only does this give you an overview of your short-term priorities, but it also gives you a chance to check how much 'free' time you have left. You know how time gets filled with routine tasks, urgent problems, other people's demands on you, last-minute meetings and all the rest of it. So check you have plenty of time still available. If not:

- See if you can cancel or absent yourself from any meetings.
- Delegate any tasks you have scheduled for yourself.
- Reorganize your diary so it is more streamlined – reschedule those two meetings at the Hull office for the same day, or put two half-day planning sessions into the diary for the same day, freeing up a whole day elsewhere.

Whatever you do, though, do not be tempted to cancel or squeeze down any time allocated for key tasks, unless they can be delegated effectively. These are your raison d'être. The problem is, they are often the tasks it is logistically easiest to move or cancel. So never lose sight of your objective. The most successful managers are the ones who understand that these tasks are their absolute top priorities.

WEEKLY PLANNING

This is where you plan in all those other tasks that have to be done sometime. It should only take five minutes each Monday morning. You need to set aside time during the week for:

- delegating and monitoring delegated tasks
- dealing with correspondence and e-mails
- catching up with phone calls
- dealing with miscellaneous tasks
- being available on the phone (an assistant can put off callers during busy periods by saying that you will definitely be free to answer their calls on Wednesday afternoon, for example)

- being available face-to-face (a permanent open-door policy is a licence to interrupt you; better to schedule time when your staff and colleagues know you will be available so they don't need to bother you otherwise unless it's really urgent).

You might want to schedule some of these more than once in the week. Rather than being available on the phone or face-to-face for an hour once a week, it might be better to have two half-hour sessions so nobody has to wait more than a couple of days to pin you down. Or be available for the last fifteen minutes of every day.

DAILY PLANNING

At the start of each day, decide how you will allocate any spare time (yes, with this system you may actually have spare time – well, at the planning stage anyway). You should aim to have a walkabout every day (OK, you won't always succeed, but if you don't try you'll never succeed) among your staff so that you are in touch with them, and seen to be in touch (known as managing by walking about). You'll also have urgent tasks to deal with from writing up a brief report to making phone calls and dealing with problems. So decide when you'll do these.

Start the day by drawing up a 'to-do' list. This lists all the things you are going to fit in between your scheduled tasks, meetings and so on. You may find it helps to list phone calls separately; it is much more efficient to do them all at once if you can. So your list might read:

Phone

John Surrey, BTC (8812 6543)

Mike re report

Liz Kennedy

Robin South, Plimley Bros (01234 987654)

To do

Check up on Hedges account

Check Meg re proposal research

Prices from Onyx

Review schedule for exhibition

E-mail Paul re exhibition stand

8 do it

As you work through your groups in order of priority – according to your schedule – you are dumping, delegating or deferring everything you can. However, there will still be some tasks left over in most groups: those you have to do now, or almost now (in other words, too soon to defer). These might include phone calls and e-mails, documents to read, decisions to make, papers to approve, cheques to sign, and operational or personnel problems to solve. A mishmash of easy and difficult, quick and time-consuming tasks.

Essentially, you simply have to work through these as fast and effectively as you can, having cleared any potential interruptions out of the way. However, there are a couple of tips to help speed up the process:

- **Some kinds of brief tasks will keep cropping up throughout the groups. For example, there will probably be several e-mails to send, or several phone calls to make. It is usually much more efficient to do all these related tasks at the same time, so save them all up and have a blitz on e-mails when you get to the end of the groups, or**

thinking smart

KEEP IN TOUCH

Making responses to people can sometimes be staved off if you're pushed for time by simply acknowledging their call, letter or e-mail. Send them a note or an e-mail that says 'Thanks for your letter/e-mail/call. I am giving it some thought and will get back to you in the next few days.' Make sure you do get back to them, of course, but you've bought yourself two or three days' grace.

sign off all the invoices at once. Of course, a few may need doing earlier – some other tasks may depend on the outcome of a particular phone call perhaps – but use your common sense and group together what you can.

- **If any task in a group is dependent on any other, pick this up swiftly and make sure the primary task gets done first. If it takes time – maybe you need to get someone to call you back with a piece of information – get the ball rolling promptly.**

MAKING LISTS

You may well find that you need to make lists of things to do as you go through your workload. If you are working in your office, obviously you can't do, here and now, any tasks that require you to be

It is much more efficient to do related tasks at the same time

on the shop floor – updating yourself on equipment problems, or talking to the production manager face-to-face – or at another branch, or down at the shops looking through your competitors' products.

Likewise, if you are working from home, you don't necessarily have access to everything you need, and may need a list of things to do as soon as you get back to the office. Or you might be working in the evening, and can't do anything that requires you to get hold of other people before tomorrow. You will also be saving up lists of phone calls, e-mails and so on to do together at the end of your clear-out session.

Anything you delay for more than a few hours should go into your diary, as we've seen. But there's no point writing every phone call in tomorrow morning's diary when you could simply write 'work through phone calls' and then make a separate list as you go along.

All the tasks to go on the list should already be written down somewhere in the relevant pile of papers, so your list might consist of a pile of notes and papers. But many people find their minds are clearer when their work is looking neater. If this is you, you may be happier composing a single list, and attaching to it any relevant papers to which you may need to refer.

DON'T GET CAUGHT

Sometimes you need to call someone who you know is likely to trap you on the phone. If you are one of those people who is under-assertive about extricating yourself, call when you're pretty sure they will be out and leave a voicemail message instead.

Some people dread the look of a long list – it seems like such a lot to get through. If you need a psychological boost, put the following things at the top of your list:

- **something you will enjoy doing**
- **something that will be really quick**
- **a task you have already done.**

If you tick off each job as you do it, you'll find that almost instantly you'll have these first three items ticked. That will make you feel you're really cracking on.

Making decisions

Most of the tasks you have to do will not necessarily be difficult; it's just a matter of getting around to them – as you now have. But the one

Anything you delay for more than a few hours should go into your diary

category of tasks that most managers have piled up on their desks when time is getting the better of them is anything that requires a decision. The companion volume to this, *Fast Thinking: Decisions*, will help you to prevent this kind of pile-up. But in the meantime, here's a flash guide to making decisions fast.

Your current aim is to clear your work backlog. Now is not the time to make major decisions such as who to sack, or whether to switch to outsourcing your entire accounts function. If any decision of this magnitude needs to be made (and you're unlikely to be making it alone), schedule some time to do it later. At the moment we're concerned with more everyday – if important – decisions such as:

- **What level of raise should we give to a member of staff?**
- **Which model of van should we switch to as our fleet vehicle?**
- **Which of the applicants should we offer the telephone sales assistant job to?**
- **Should we go ahead with the plan to extend the car parking area?**
- **Should I accept a subordinate's proposal?**

These are the kind of decisions that can pile up on your desk … until now. Of course, you don't only want to make these decisions fast, you also want to make them right. The ability to make good decisions fast is one of the cornerstones of success for managers. So what are the techniques for achieving it?

Many decisions are so easy that you barely notice you're making them: what time will you hold this meeting? Who will you delegate this task to? Others are straightforward because the answer is clear: there may have been only one really good applicant for the job, so there's no need to agonize over who to offer it to. But these, of course, are not the decisions you have been putting off.

Here are the key considerations to help you make any tricky decision you find lying in wait among your pile of papers:

- **Should you be making this decision? Sometimes we put off decisions because we know deep down that someone else should be making them, or that the whole premise of the decision is wrong. For example, how can you choose which proposal to accept for designing the launch of a new product when you have serious doubts about whether the product should be launched at all? We may not want to take the decision because we know that we don't really have enough information to judge it. So remedy the problem – pass the decision on, instigate discussion about your reservations regarding the new product, ask for more information before you make the decision.**

The ability to make good decisions fast is one of the cornerstones of success

- What is your objective? Objective setting *again*? Yep, 'fraid so. Determine the core aim of taking this decision – what you intend to achieve by it. For example, your objective might be to pay your staff an affordable salary that reflects the value of the job they do and motivates them to do even better. Or it might be to ensure ample parking for staff and visitors within a certain budget. You cannot know what the right decision is if you don't know what you are aiming to achieve.
- Collect all the data you can. As I've already mentioned, you may need to collect more information. When the time comes to make the decision, make sure you are not missing relevant data. If you don't know what your staff member's performance has been like over the past few months, how can you meet your objective of ensuring that their salary reflects the value of the job they do?
- Don't make a decision you can't implement. Rule out all options that can't be achieved. There's no point deciding to extend the car park if there's nowhere for it to go without huge landscaping works, which will mean spending a fortune you haven't got in the budget.

thinking smart

ASK ADVICE IF IT WILL HELP

Why not call someone else up? Others may have been through a similar decision-making process before, or may have more experience in this area than you. You don't have to take their advice, but you can feed it into the system.

- **Listen to your intuition.** Many people mock intuition, and others simply don't trust it. Generally it is not wise to make a decision on instinct alone, but if you have all the data and it doesn't point to a clear answer, intuition will often tell you which way to go. So listen to it as you would to an experienced advisor.
- **Don't force a decision unnecessarily.** Just because you have this load of work to clear off your desk, it isn't necessarily wise to make every decision now. If things aren't going to change, and no new data will turn up, you'll be no nearer to a decision in a month than you are now. But if the decision isn't urgent and you feel that more time will help in some way – if only so that you can sleep on it and clear your head – there's no point taking the decision just because it's there.
- **When you have to make a decision, do it.** If a decision needs to be taken now (if not last week), you *must* learn to do it. You may never have every last piece of information to guarantee a perfect decision, but speed is important too. A correct decision taken too slowly may be worse than a less perfect decision taken promptly. One of the biggest bars to successful decision-making is the temptation to weigh up all the pros and cons endlessly. But the dynamic manager must learn to say 'Enough!' Better to make an adequate decision than none at all. Sometimes every option has its drawbacks, but you still have to pick one of them.
- **Be committed to your decision.** Once you have made your decision, you must stick to it. And that includes being seen to stick to it. When your staff member rails against

One of the biggest bars to successful decision-making is the temptation to weigh up all the pros and cons endlessly

TOSS A COIN

If there's really nothing to choose between two options, why not simply toss a coin? If you've looked at all the arguments and there's that little between them, it probably doesn't matter which decision you make – so just make one.

your decision not to give them the raise they wanted, don't waver. If that was the right decision you can be sympathetic, but don't allow yourself to be swayed.

- **Be prepared to sell your decision to other people. The right decisions are not always the most popular ones. So be ready to persuade other people that even if it's not what they want, this is the right decision. They may have wanted better car parking or a different model of fleet vehicle, but be ready to explain why this is the best course.**

Following these guidelines you should find it simple to make those decisions that are cluttering up your work pile. And in the process you'll be exercising a vital management skill.

READING

One of the real stomach-sinking ingredients of most piles of work is material that needs to be read. Those thick wodges of reports, proposals, research documents, publications, minutes of meetings you didn't attend, and all the rest of it. How on earth are you going to wade through all that in the few short hours you have? You're not – face it.

Do you imagine that every other manager, including your boss and your board of directors, doesn't have exactly the same problem? Of course they do. So what's their solution? There are two options. One of them – in the long term – is to learn speed reading. You haven't really got time to do that today, but I thoroughly recommend it if you regularly have a lot of material to read. (You'll find a fast thinker's guide to speed reading in the companion volume to this one, *Fast Thinking: Finding Facts*.)

The second option is to read only what you have to. You don't have to read every word of every document sitting in your in-tray, so don't feel you must. Here are a few tips for minimizing your reading:

thinking smart

BEDTIME READING

You obviously have to do some reading, even if you don't have to read everything that lands on your desk. So schedule some reading time into your diary each week for catching up.

- Just because someone gives you something to read, you don't automatically have to read it. *You* decide whether it warrants your attention. Measure it against your core objective – will reading this really help you to achieve it?
- Read the contents page and introduction to a book first and you may find it tells you all you need (or that you don't need to read it at all).
- Ask other people to read articles or documents for you, and give you a brief verbal or written report on them. They can highlight or clip any short passages they feel you should read.
- Many books, reports, proposals and so on have short summaries or chapter summaries. This is often all you need to read.
- If there is no summary, a well-written document often has a summarizing final paragraph to each section at least. Try reading only the first and last paragraphs of each section. This should give you enough information to see which sections you need to read more thoroughly and which you can skip with impunity.
- If you subscribe to trade publications or papers, just identify the top two or three most relevant articles. Read these, and throw the rest away.

You've done well to get this far, and the only challenge left is to avoid finding yourself in this situation again. Follow the 'For next time' guidelines in this book and you should find that when it comes to work overload, there isn't a next time.

thinking smart

THE ONE-PAGE RULE

Make it a rule among everyone who works for you that every report, proposal or other document must have a summary attached which is no longer than a single side of A4 paper. No memo or internal e-mail should exceed this length either.

The moment a piece of paper reaches your desk, you should deal with it

for next time

In theory, you should never accumulate a pile of things to do in the first place (business theories are great, aren't they … when you want a laugh). But seriously, this one can work with a little practice and a lot of discipline. The idea is that we all push the same pieces of paper around our desks for days or even weeks before we finally deal with them (all right then, for months sometimes).

The solution is to have a firm rule that the moment a piece of paper reaches us, we deal with it and then get it off the desk. And there are only four options for dealing with it.

1 **Bin it.** You know all those papers you've just sorted out and dumped? How many of them could just as well have been dumped the minute they arrived on your desk all those weeks ago? Learning to identify rubbish at first glance is the smart thinker's approach.

2 **File it.** We've talked about having files for major projects from the outset. So if paperwork that needs keeping doesn't go into your archive file, it can at least go into your active 'presentation' file, or your 'budget' file, or your 'personnel' file.

3 **Pass it on.** If this can be passed on to a colleague or delegated to someone, do it now, instead of storing it on your desk for a fortnight and then doing it.

4 **Act on it.** Don't build up a pending file – act on everything you can immediately. If you don't, you simply build up a backlog (and we know all about that) so that you are continually acting on last week's or last month's paperwork. Now you've finally caught up, stay ahead of the game.

clearing a work overload in half a day

If you have only half a day to sort out your entire backlog of work, relax. You've got plenty of time. Even the heftiest overload can be straightened out in three or four hours. The first thing to do is to read this book right through. It'll only take you about an hour, and everything you need to know is in here.

You'll want to go through the stages in the book in terms of organizing the work, prioritizing and sorting through the groups, but you'll have to make sure the really urgent tasks get tackled today – schedule them first before you start to work through the groups. That way, however short the time is, the essentials will be covered.

After that, you simply need to go through the stages set out, but bear a few points in mind:

- **Setting your objective, organizing the work into groups and prioritizing your workload are essential stages: do not be tempted to skip them. In the long run they will save you far more time than they take up, and they will ensure the work is dealt with effectively.**
- **You may need to delegate a lot of work, so don't be hesitant about whether anyone else can do it. If you have a good team working with you – large or small – most tasks can be delegated. If you're not in the habit of delegating freely you may have to learn a new habit fast.**
- **Just because you can't delegate a whole task, it doesn't mean you can't delegate part of it. Maybe you have to remain actively involved in preparing for next week's exhibition, but someone else can liaise with the stand designers and the printers for you.**
- **You are also going to have to defer a fair amount of work. The important thing is to schedule it for as soon as possible, before it all gets out of hand again, but be realistic about how much you can fit in. There *will* be interruptions and emergencies, and if you haven't allowed for these you will quickly slip behind and become demoralized.**

just because you can't delegate a whole task, it doesn't mean you can't delegate part of it

If your half day is an evening, you have the advantage that you are less likely to be interrupted. On the other hand, it will be hard to get hold of other people. So make yourself a list of things to do as soon as the rest of the world is back in circulation. Start work early in the morning and get one of tomorrow's jobs out of the way before anyone else gets into the office. Use the time that this clears later in the day to make all your phone calls.

You should find that half a day is ample time to get on top of a backlog of work. It won't all be done by the end of the session, but it will all be in hand and back under control. So don't panic; just relax and get started. Before you know it things will be looking a whole lot more manageable.

You should find that half a day is ample time to get on top of a backlog of work

clearing a work overload in an hour

You've managed to clear an hour – one single, solitary hour – to tackle several weeks' or even months' pile-up. You obviously do one of those jobs where the speed of life has overtaken you. Let's be realistic for a moment. Can you really get all this work done and out of the way in an hour? Of course you can't. So why have we put a page in this book headed 'Clearing a work overload in an hour'?

The answer is that although you can't do the work in an hour, you can prepare the ground for doing it. And that's all you need. So how do you go about it?

- **Don't even think about urgent tasks for the time being – they'll have to be subject to whatever system you operate all the rest of the time. Deal with them in the usual fashion *after* this one-hour blitz.**
- **Read Chapter 7 on deferring tasks – you're going to need it.**
- **Read Chapter 1 on creating time. Don't panic: they're the only chapters you have to read for now.**
- **On the basis of what these two chapters tell you, create an hour as soon as possible – bedtime would do nicely – to read this book right through.**
- **Now schedule at least half a day, but preferably a whole day, to put into action the contents of this book. Make sure you fit this time into the next seven days *no matter what*. You may well prefer to start work an hour early each day for the next week (I know you probably already have to get up half an hour before you go to bed), or to give up an evening to clear the workload.**

If you have any of your hour left at the end of this, feel free to sit and twiddle your thumbs. Or start reading the book now. You may not have your work overload cleared by the end of today, but you'll be making an essential start on it, and with a touch of fast thinking it will be clear by the end of next week. So relax!